BLUENOSE
& BLUENOSE II

R. KEITH McLAREN

Bluenose and Bluenose II

Text and Photographs: R. Keith McLaren

Editor: John Robert Colombo

Designer: Gerard Williams

Typesetter: Kerr Graphics

Publisher: Anthony Hawke

Printer: Heritage Co. Ltd.

Copyright © 1981 By R. Keith McLaren
All Rights Reserved.
ISBN 0-88882-042-9

Hounslow Press
A Division of Anthony R. Hawke Limited
124 Parkview Avenue
Willowdale, Ontario, Canada
M2N 3Y5

Printed in Canada

1. *The* Bluenose *off the Isle of Wight, 1935.*

2. *Fishing Schooners, Lunenburg, Nova Scotia, 1926.*

Can the Bluenose Sail?

Once Captain Walters was asked if the Bluenose could really sail as fast as was claimed.

"Can she sail?" queried the Captain. "Man, she can sail like a comet. Did I ever tell you how she beat the Dog star in a race across the sky?

"'Twas a fine night and a boy was at the wheel. He hadn't very much experience and needed a bit of watching; so as I was going below for a while I said to him, 'Boy, keep her head on the Dog star there and ye'll be all right.'

"'Aye, aye, sir,' says he.

"Being down below for a while I left the boy to his own devices and presently he hailed with the trace of excitement: 'Hi, skipper, come up and find me another star . . . I've passed that one.'"

Shelbourne Coast Guard, November 30, 1939

BLUENOSE
Queen of the North Atlantic Fishing Fleet

3. *Close hauled and laying down to it,* Bluenose *in her best racing form.*

No longer are the North American fishing grounds crowded with the tall spars and sleek hulls of the Canadian and American fishing schooners. Once there were hundreds, now there are none, but the heritage remains. Men still fish the same waters today, but with boats and equipment that is so completely different from that of their forefathers. Of this past age, one fishing schooner caught and held the imagination of the world; she was the *Bluenose.* Her life became legend in a short period of time, and her passing marked the end of an era. From 1921 until 1938, the *Bluenose* built a reputation that is unsurpassed in Canadian maritime history. The following is an account of her career as a fisherman and as a racer in the International Fisherman's Race where she was crowned Queen of the North Atlantic Fishing Fleet.

During the early part of this century, the fishing fleets of Canada's Maritime provinces and America's New England States operated under sail. Motor-driven vessels were making headway in the fishing industry previous to 1920, but due to high cost of engine installation the industry continued to use the still productive and cheaper method of sail propulsion. Marine architects were called upon to design faster sailing vessels to compete with this new mechanized era. In Canada, since the fish trade was mostly engaged in salted fish products which could sustain long periods in holds before delivery, boat designs were towards a larger vessel with greater carrying capacity. In the United States, fishermen were becoming involved in the fresh-fish market; consequently, their designs were for a smaller vessel than their Canadian counterpart, speed being the most important factor. Their stays on the Banks would be shorter, and more trips were necessitated by the swift delivery of fresh fish. Both designs demanded that the vessels carry great amounts of sail, because both wished to get their goods to market in as fast a time as possible and have quick returns to the Banks. Beyond the carrying capacity and speed, the vessels had to be stout enough to weather the rigorous life of working the North Atlantic fishing grounds where the

4. *Dories were drifted behind the schooner so they could be dispersed evenly over the fishing grounds.*

5. *Atlantic Cod, the mainstay of the schooner fishermen.*

6. *On board a fishing schooner during a mid-winter run to the Banks.*

weather is considered by many the most punishing in the world. Boats had to be constructed that could stand the constant barrage of rough weather that would be expected each year off the Banks.

The life of a Banks fisherman was not to be envied. Long hours, days, and weeks would be spent in open dories which were let off a schooner over the Banks. Most schooners carried between twelve and sixteen of these small but durable craft which were manned singly or in pairs. In all types of weather men could be seen scattered over the fishing grounds handlining for cod or halibut. The catches were passed to the schooner where the fish was split, then taken to the hold to be salted. They worked long, exhausting hours each day for very little pay. Relaxation, when it came, was usually centered around the foundry stove in a crowded forecastle. After the evening meal the men found time to fill their pipes and spend a time "yarning" about local or worldly interests before going back on deck for the evening watch or climbing into a bunk for a few hours' sleep.

During this period one of the most popular subjects of interest was the America's Cup Races. Many hours in the forecastle would be spent discussing the limitations of this event. The race, begun in 1851, was a test of seamanship between the best schooners Britain and the United States had to offer. These schooners were built by members of the respective yachting fraternities and were designed specifically for racing. In 1919 one race was postponed because of mere 25-knot winds and this drew heated comments from the Banks fishermen. They complained that the race had become far too rule-bound, and the vessels competing had become far too fragile. To a saltbank sailor this wasn't a test of seamanship as he knew it. The fishermen began thinking that a better competition could be made among themselves.

Common talk of the time suggested that a race be set up on an international basis between the Canadian and American fishing fleets. Editorials in fishing publications soon caught on to the idea and promoted an international race between fishing schoon-

Conditions of the Deed of Gift
The original Race Rules that governed the International Fisherman's Race.

The Halifax Herald's International Fishermen's Trophy. The International Fishermen's Race was promoted in October, 1920, by The Halifax Herald. The trophy, emblematic of the Fishing Fleet Championship of the North Atlantic, was presented by Senator W.H. Dennis, The Halifax Herald and The Halifax Mail. **Conditions of Deed of Gift.** To All Men Greetings. Be it known that William H. Dennis, representing the proprietors of The Halifax Herald and The Halifax Mail newspapers, published in the City of Halifax, in the Province of Nova Scotia, Canada, recognizing the great importance and value of the deep sea fishing industry to the inhabitants of this Province of Nova Scotia, and realizing the necessity of the best possible type of craft being employed in the pursuit of the industry, and believing that this can best be obtained by engendering a spirit of friendly competition among the fishermen of this Province and also with the fishermen engaged in similar methods of fishing in the other Maritime Provinces of Canada, the Dominion of Newfoundland and the United States of America, has donated and placed under the control of Trustees to be named herein, a TROPHY, of which a photograph and description thereof shall be attached hereto, to be known as: **The Halifax Herald North Atlantic Fishermen's International** Trophy to be sailed for annually under the Rules and Conditions which follow, which may be added to, taken from or modified from time to time to meet changing conditions of the Industry by the Trustees herein appointed, or their successors. The said Rules or any modification

thereof being always drawn in such manner as to safeguard and continue the intention of the Donors of the Trophy, which is the development of the most practical and serviceable type of fishing schooner combined with the best sailing qualities, without sacrificing utility. For the purpose of maintaining this principle the Trustees are empowered to disqualify from all or any competition any vessel which in their opinion is of such a type or dimensions as would contravert the intention of the Donors and such decisions of the Trustees shall be final; the Trustees shall, however, do nothing which will change the spirit of the intention of the Donors, that the competitors shall be confined to vessels and crews engaged in practical commercial fishing. The Trustees in whom the control of the Trophy is vested are The Honourable The Premier of Nova Scotia, His Worship The Mayor of Halifax, Messrs. H.R. Silver, H.G. DeWolf, R.A. Corbett, H.G. Lawrence, W.J. Roue, F.W. Baldwin, Captain V.C. Johnson, being members of the original Committee; any vacancies arising to be filled by a majority vote of the remaining Trustees, who, in conference with the representatives of the Gloucester Committee in charge of the races held in the year Nineteen Hundred and, Twenty have drawn the following Rules and Regulations, which shall govern all future races until and unless good and sufficient reason arises for their modification in such manner as the Trustees may consider advisable.

Continued on the next page.

---

ers. Everyone involved in the fishing industry seemed to be in common agreement that a race between men who made their living upon the sea would be a far superior test of seamanship than that of the America's Cup Race. It was the owner of a Halifax newspaper, William H. Dennis, who finally consolidated the idea of an International Fisherman's Race by putting up a trophy for which the Canadian and American fishing fleets could compete.

The public reaction to the race was overwhelming. The papers announced that this would be the ultimate in International sailing events. "A Race For Real Sailors" it was called, and the rules for this race would be the ones the seamen knew best — the rules of the road as practised every day at sea and "not the new-fangled regulations" used by the other International Cup races. The competition would be "a demonstration that the age of sail is not ended" and the race would also illuminate the possibilities in vessel design for fisheries use.

Eliminations were held in Halifax, Nova Scotia, and Gloucester, Massachusetts, to determine which vessel in each fleet would win the right to challenge the cup. The Halifax eliminations were held on October 11, 1920. Eight boats lined up on the starting line just north of Point Pleasant Park at the breakwater. The competitors were the *Delawana, Gilbert B. Walters, Alcala, Mona Marie, Bernice Zinck, Freda M. Himmelman, Ruby L. Prentz,* and *Independence.* First across the finish line was the *Delawana* with Captain Thomas Himmelman and, second, despite a broken foretopmast, was the *Gilbert B. Walters* with Captain Angus Walters. The eliminations in Gloucester resulted in the victorious *Esperanto* with Captain Marty Welch making her way to Halifax to compete against the *Delawana* for the first International Fisherman's Trophy.

The first race was set for October 30, 1920, and Halifax prepared for the event. Visitors poured into the city from all over Canada and the United States. Headlines filled the newspapers and the schooner race became the chief topic of conversation.

Enormous crowds lined the waterfront to watch these great contenders at the start. At

1. This Trophy is being presented by the proprietors of The Halifax Herald and The Halifax Mail, as a perpetual International Championship Trophy, to be raced for annually.

2. All races for this Trophy shall be under the control and management of an International Committee of five, which shall be elected for each series of races; the Trustees will nominate the two members of the Committee to represent Nova Scotia, and the Governor of the Commonwealth of Massachusetts, in conjunction with the local United States Committee handling the race, shall name the two members of the Committee to represent United States. The Chairman of this Committee shall be named by the two members of the Committee representing the country in which the race is to be held.

3. The Race shall be sailed in the year 1921 off the Harbour of Halifax, Nova Scotia, and alternately thereafter off Gloucester (or a course in Massachusetts Bay to be mutually agreed upon by the International Committee in charge of the Race) and off Halifax, Nova Scotia. The dates on which the races are to be sailed shall be decided by the International Committee, but shall be fixed so as not to unduly interfere with the business in which the craft are engaged.

4. The only vessels which can compete for the trophy shall be bona fide fishing vessels, which have been engaged in commercial deep sea fishing for at least one season previous to the race. A fishing season for the purpose of these rules is considered as extending from the month of April to September, and any vessel competing must have actually sailed from her last port of departure for the Fishing Banks not later than April thirtieth in any year and have remained on the fishing grounds in all weather as customary, until the month of September, excepting necessary returns to port for landing cargo and refitting. Fishing Banks shall mean all off-shore Banks, such as George's, Western, Grand, etc., and vessels engaged in shore fishing and making port in bad weather shall not be eligible.

5. The Captain and Crew of each competing vessel shall be bona fide fishermen, actively engaged in deep sea fishing, and the number of the crew shall be fixed by the International Committee. A list of the crew of each vessel and substitutes therefor shall be forwarded to the International Committee one week before the Series takes place, and each vessel competing shall be furnished with a copy of the Crew List of the opposing vessel or vessels.

6. All competing vessels shall be propelled by sails only and must comply with the following measurements and conditions:

(a) Overall length: Not to exceed one hundred and forty-five (145) feet, from outside of stem to outside of taffrail.

(b) Water line length, in racing trim, not to exceed one hundred and twelve (112) feet from outside of stem at point of submersion to point of submersion at the stern.

(c) Draught of vessel in racing trim shall not exceed sixteen (16) feet from the lowest point of the keel to the racing water line, measured vertically.

(d) No outside ballast shall be used.

(e) Inside ballast shall consist of any material of a not greater specific gravity than iron.

(f) Competing vessels shall race with the same spars, including booms and gaffs (which must all be solid), as are used in fishing.

(g) Competing vessels must be of the usual type, both in form and construction, sail plan and rigging, as customary in the fishing industry, and any radical departure therefrom may be regarded as a freak and eliminated.

7. (a) The sails used in racing shall be made of the ordinary commercial duck of the same weight and texture as generally used in this class of vessel and shall have been used at least one season in fishing.

(b) Sails to be used are Mainsail, Foresail, two Jibs (including Jumbo), Jib Topsail, Fore and Main Gaff Topsails and fisherman's Staysail.

(c) The total sail area, not including fisherman's Staysail, to be no greater than eighty percent (80%) of the square of the water line length, in racing trim, as expressed in square feet. This stipulation not to apply to vessels built previous to the 1920 Races, but such existing vessels shall not increase their sail area to exceed 80% of the square of the water line if it does not already do so.

(d) The combined area of the mainsail and Main Gaff Topsail shall not be more than fifty percent (50%) of the maximum total sail area, as provided in the preceding subsection "c".

8. Mainsail: By the universal rule for mainsails, with the exception that the "B" of the formulae shall be measured from the after-side of the mainmast to the outer clew iron hole.

Main gaff topsail: Universal rule.

Foresail and fore gaff topsail: By the universal rule for actual measurement of the sails used and not a percentage of space between the masts.

Head sails: Universal rule for Head Sails.

If more than one Staysail or Jibtopsail are on the vessel they must be of the same area and only one can be set at a time.

9. No ballast shall be taken on or put off the competing vessels during the Series and no ballast shall be shifted after the Fifteen Minute Preparatory Gun is fired before each Race.

10. The International Committee shall have power to arrange all details of the Races in accordance with the Deed of Gift, and shall appoint such Sub-Committees as may be necessary to properly carry them out.

11. The Sailing Committee shall be a sub-committee, appointed by the International Committee, and shall be an independent body having no financial interest in the competing vessels. They will lay out the courses for each Series, decide the Course to be sailed for each Race, make the necessary sailing regulations and have them carried out.

12. The courses laid down by the sailing committee shall not be less than thirty-five or more than forty nautical miles in length and be so arranged as to provide windward and leeward work. The time limit of each Race shall be nine hours. There shall be no handicap or time allowance, each vessel shall sail on its merits.

13. The trophy shall be awarded to and remain in the possession for one year of the Vessel winning Two out of Three Races over Courses as laid down by the sailing committee each year, and a responsible person or corporation representing the Owners of the winning vessel shall give to the Trustees of the Trophy an official receipt therefor, together with a Bond for $500.00, obligating them to return the Trophy to the Trustees previous to the next Race, or to replace the Trophy if it becomes lost or destroyed through accident or otherwise; and to return same to the Trustees if it has not been raced for during a period of five years.

14. The total cash prizes awarded in connection with this Race in any one year shall not exceed the sum of Five Thousand Dollars ($5,000) for each Series and the distribution of the money shall be decided by the International Committee. The money for these prizes to be provided by the Committee representing the country in which the race is held.

If for any reason there should be no International Competition for this Trophy for any period of five consecutive years it shall be within the power of the Trustees to make such use of the Trophy as they may consider advisable in connection with the development of the Fishing Industry in the Province of Nova Scotia.

IN WITNESS WHEREOF we have hereunto set our hands and affixed our seals this 23rd day of March, in the year of Our Lord One Thousand Nine Hundred and Twenty-One A.D.

(Sgd)   W.H. DENNIS,
                For the Proprietors of The Halifax
                Herald and The Halifax Mail.

(Sgd)   H.R. SILVER,
                For the Trustees.

7. *Launching of* Bluenose *on March 26, 1921, in Lunenburg, Nova Scotia.*

08:45 the fifteen-minute gun was signaled and a code flag was raised to indicate which course would be used. The vessels slowly moved themselves into position. At 08:55 the five-minute gun was sounded and the boats sailed forward towards the starting line, timing their speed to hit the line when the race-start signal was given. At 09:00 the race officially began. The *Esperanto* took immediate control of the lead position and held on to it until crossing the finish line almost twenty minutes ahead of *Delawana*. Hope was not lost on the Canadian contender for it was a best-out-of-three event. The second race on November 1 was much closer, but the *Esperanto* proved the better sailor by defeating the *Delawana* across the finish by seven minutes, fifteen seconds. The American vessel sailed home to Gloucester with the prize money and the coveted Trophy.

Nova Scotians were shocked and dismayed to be beaten so soundly by the Americans, so plans were quickly drawn up to build another schooner for the following year's competition. A vessel that would be acceptable to compete in the International Fisher-man's Race had to meet conditions specified in the "Deed of Gift," which governed the disposition of the Trophy. Since the most important requirement of the race was that the contestants be *"bona-fide* fishermen," the primary function of the vessel had to be fishing, not racing. Above all, the boat had to earn a living the rest of the year and prove that she was economically sound as a fishing vessel.

A young naval architect, W. J. Roue, was commissioned to design a fishing schooner for the competition. The product was the schooner *Bluenose*, a fine, sleek-looking craft. She was built at the Smith and Rhuland Yard in Lunenburg, Nova Scotia. One alteration made during construction that caused some comment was the raising of the forecastle head by eighteen inches to facilitate more head room for the crew, but no evidence shows that this improved the speed of the vessel; only possibly did it make her deck drier forward. The *Bluenose* was launched on March 26, 1921, in good time for her to put in a season fishing on the Banks and qualify her for the races in the fall.

8. *Schooner* Mayflower *was considered too yacht-like in appearance to compete in the International* Fisherman's Race, and this caused a controversy which almost ended the series.

The *Bluenose* was financed at a cost of $35,000 by Captain Angus Walters and four Halifax businessmen who formed the Bluenose Schooner Company. She immediately proved to be a successful venture. In her early trials she seemed a handy enough vessel under the capable command of Captain Walters, and during the first season fishing on the Banks she brought in 4,200 quintals (112 lbs. to a quintal) of fish, a highly respectable amount.

Like the Canadians, the shipyards in the New England states were building new schooners. A new vessel had to be found for the upcoming competition, because the American champion, *Esperanto*, sank while fishing off Sable Island in June, 1921. Two of the new schooners were the *Yankee* and the *Mayflower*. The *Yankee*, unfortunately, turned out poorly, as her trials soon proved. She could not handle sail well and had to have engines installed to make her economical.

The *Mayflower*, designed by Starling Burgess, sported a yacht-like appearance with wire running rigging, a dolphin striker, and a slightly rakish design. Although she did put in a qualifying season on the Banks, the International Race committee considered her primarily a racing rather than a fishing vessel, and this contravened the conditions provided under the "Deed of Gift." Their decision to disqualify her from the race caused great controversy which at one point threatened to cancel the entire series. The committee in Gloucester finally adhered to the decision, but only after bitter argument.

The 1921 eliminations were held in October. In Gloucester a small, sprightly schooner named *Elsie* won out in a race against four other competitors: The *Elsie G. Silvia, Ralph Brown, Phillip P. Manta,* and *Arthur James.* In Halifax nine vessels were ready at the starting line for the 1921 eliminations. Two races determined the challenger of the cup, one on October 15 and the other on the 17th. The *Bluenose* became the unquestioned winner after beating the *Canadia* by four minutes in the first race and by seventeen minutes in the second. The other vessels in the race were the *Donald J.*

9. *All crew aboard the* Bluenose *were to keep their heads down below the weather rail while sailing close hauled.*

11. Elsie, *the first American schooner to race against* Bluenose *in 1921, was small and fast, but no match for the larger Canadian schooner.*

Corkum, Delawana, J. Duffy, Independence, Senora, Alcala, and the *Uda R. Corkum.* The *Bluenose* had proven to be as successful a racer as she was a fisherman.

The success of the *Bluenose* was largely due to the capable captain and her excellent crew. *The Halifax Herald,* October 24, 1921, commented on Captain Walters, "Aboard and during the race he is a martinet for discipline and order. The owner of a head that shows above the weather rail knows about it in a manner that leaves no room for back talk. He did his commanding with the aid of a megaphone and he has a caustic tongue. He is a driver from gun to gun." His crew were seasoned "salt-bankers" that knew their trade; no less than nine were captains of their own boats.

Captain Marty Welsh of the American Schooner, *Elsie,* was a very capable skipper and his crew, like the crew of the *Bluenose,* were largely men who captained their own boats. Furthermore, the *Elsie* had a reputation of being swift for Captain Welsh astonished listeners by telling them of hauling his log at 13 knots on his trip up

10. *Captain Angus Walters, Master of* Bluenose.

12. & 13. Elsie *losing her foretopmast in the first race of the 1921 International Fisherman's Cup series.*

from Gloucester.

The first race on the 22nd was won by the *Bluenose*. She had gained the advantage during the first leg and kept it through to the end. Unfortunately, the *Elsie* lost her foretopmast during the latter part of the race, losing the use of her foretopsail and jibtopsail. Captain Walters, in the interests
5 of keeping the race "fair and square," doused his own foretopsail, but the *Bluenose* was already well in the lead and crossed the finish line thirteen minutes and fifteen seconds ahead of the *Elsie*.

The second race was a far more exciting contest. *Elsie* crossed the starting line several boat-lengths ahead of the *Bluenose* and held on to this lead, passing each mark half a minute ahead of her opponent. It was not until the fourth mark was passed and the windward race began from Shut-In Island Bell to the Inner Automatic Buoy that the *Bluenose* forged ahead. In her best sailing form, she drove down relentlessly upon the *Elsie* and took the race by eleven minutes. The crowds cheered from the shore as *Bluenose* flew across the finish line. Nova

Scotians were jubilant. The *Bluenose* had proved to be a champion and had brought the International Fisherman's Trophy back home.

Through the winter, plans and construction began in various ports in the United States in hopes of having a brand-new challenger ready for the next year's race. In Essex, Massachusetts, a fine, new schooner called the *Puritan* seemed to be a likely contender for the Fisherman's Race. During her trials and impromptu races she was found to be a very fast sailor, but her career was cut short. During a trip to the Banks in June, she hit the north-west bar of Sable Island and was lost. The *Henry Ford*, also built in Essex, was finished almost a month later than the *Puritan*. Her late launching and fitting out didn't allow the boat to put in a full season on the fishing grounds, as the Fisherman's Race rules demanded, but she fell in with every other condition specified in the "Deed of Gift," so the Race committee decided it would be fair to allow the *Ford* to enter the year's competition.

The ruling on the *Ford* upset the owners

14. *Shortly after launching, the American schooner* Henry Ford *slipped away in the fog and was found* *later high and dry on a sand bar. Fortunately no damage was reported.*

of the previously disqualified *Mayflower*. They tried to enter the competition a second time and were again rejected. The owners felt their vessel had more than proven herself to be a *bona-fide* "fisherman," but the race committee refused to alter their former
6 decision, as further "evidence" cited the title on the construction plans, which called the
7 *Mayflower* a "schooner-yacht." The *Mayflower* reluctantly accepted the decision, but sent out a challenge to the winner of the 1922 race to compete against the *Mayflower* in a separate race.

The Americans held their eliminations on October 12, 13 and 14, and the *Henry Ford* under Captain Clayton Moissey won against the *Elizabeth Howard*, *Yankee*, and *L.A. Dutton*. The Canadian eliminations were held on October 7, 9 and 10, with the *Bluenose* competing against the *Canadia*, *Mahaska*, and *Margaret K. Smith*. During the first race, the *Bluenose* showed an astonishing display of speed. Leading the boats at the start, Walters made an error in navigation and passed the Inner Automatic Buoy on the starboard hand instead of to

port. Following quickly upon the heels of the *Bluenose* was the *Mahaska*, making the same mistake, while the *Canadia* and *Margaret K. Smith* took the lead by passing on the proper side of the buoy. Recognizing his mistake, Walters immediately proceeded to correct it, yelling, "Spit on your hands
8 and never say die, boys," and he swung the big vessel around to repass the buoy on the proper side. By the time she had come around, the *Canadia* was in the lead almost a mile ahead, with the *Smith* close behind. With a combination of the vessel's speed and Captain Walters' fierce determination to win, the *Bluenose* narrowed down the distance, passed the *Smith*, and finally caught up with the *Canadia* and forged ahead to cross the finish line seven minutes ahead of the rest. Due to light winds, the next two contests were not finished within
9 the time limit and were called "No Race" by the committee, but because of the superb performance of the *Bluenose* during the first race, it was decided that she be named the defender.

Four races were held in Gloucester in

15. Bluenose, close-hauled and heading for home,
wins the 1922 International Fisherman's Trophy.

16. All sail up and drawing as the Henry Ford *pushes
on toward the finish line in an unsuccessful attempt to
capture the 1922 title.*

17. *The* Columbia *was considered the fastest competitor to race against* Bluenose, *but due to a dispute over* *regulations the 1923 series was left incompleted.*

1922. The first was unofficial; the sailing committee cancelled the race due to false starts of both vessels, but the Captains of the *Ford* and *Bluenose* decided to race anyway, ignoring both the recall signal and a Coast Guard boat sent out to bring them back. The *Ford* took an easy win beating *Bluenose* by almost twenty-two minutes, and although Captain Walters told the committee that it was a fair race and to "tally one up for Clayte," the race committee wouldn't hear of it and declared the race unofficial.

The second race on the 23rd was won by the *Henry Ford*, beating the *Bluenose* by two-and-one-half minutes. Two days later the *Bluenose* beat the *Ford*, but the citizens of Gloucester were outraged at what they considered an unfair contest, because the *Ford* had lost her foretopmast in the event. The Race Committee considered the protest and decided that the wind was not strong enough to warrant a broken topmast and gave the race to the *Bluenose*. The next day the final and deciding race was won by the *Bluenose* by almost eight minutes. The *Bluenose* retained the Fisherman's Trophy

and received a cash prize of $3,000. The defeated *Henry Ford* won $2,000.

The promised race with the *Mayflower* never happened, because at the end of the 1922 series a *Bluenose* crewman, Bert Demone, fell in the harbour and drowned. The *Bluenose* crewman had no desire to engage in another race after this mishap and left for Lunenburg in mourning.

In September 1923 the fishing fleets had just finished another season on the Banks and were preparing themselves for the next international series. The Americans had built another schooner in the spring called the *Columbia*, which was designed by Burgess and Paine and built in Essex. She had put in a qualifying season on the Banks and was ready for the race. After winning a last-minute challenge from the *Henry Ford*, the *Columbia* sailed to Halifax to race against the *Bluenose*, now established as the Cup's defender.

The first race, run on October 29, 1923, was one of the most exciting of all the series. The *Bluenose* led at the start by thirty seconds, and increased the lead to two-and-

18. *This section of an aerial film strip shows the* Bluenose *pulling away from* Columbia *moments after the two collided in the 1923 race. This incident was not protested, but caused the sailing committee to impose a new set of regulations.*

one-half minutes by the second mark, the Outer Automatic Buoy. Captain Ben Pine drove the *Columbia* as hard as he dare, and during the windward race from the second mark to the Sambro Light Ship he succeeded in closing the distance between him and the *Bluenose*. As both vessels passed the third mark, they were neck and neck, with the *Bluenose* to windward and on a course for the shoal off Chebucto Head. It was a dangerous course to follow, but the *Columbia* lay directly alongside and Captain Pine was not about to give up the advantage by falling off to leeward. They passed Bell Rock Buoy to landward and tension grew as the *Bluenose* edged closer to the white water of the shoals. Captain Walters had little choice but to force the *Columbia* over to give the *Bluenose* more sea room. The *Columbia* would not give an inch as the two great schooners closed in together. The *Bluenose*'s bowsprit brushed up against the *Columbia*'s forward shrouds and caught up on a halyard, and for about a minute the *Bluenose* was actually towing the *Columbia*, until the vessels parted company and the

Bluenose inched ahead. She gained the lead of about one minute by the fourth mark and won the race by the small margin of one minute, twenty seconds. Surprisingly, no protests were lodged by either vessel, but the sailing committee immediately wrote out a set of Special Rules (the 1923 Rules) to prevent such an incident from happening again.

The second race occurred on November 1. In another close contest, the *Bluenose* held the lead and won the race by two minutes, forty-five seconds, but it was not a clear win. The *Bluenose* had ignored the new special rule pertaining to the passing of buoys and had passed Lighthouse Buoy on the wrong side, to landward. Walters argued that the buoy wasn't a distance marker, only a channel buoy, and his deviation didn't affect the distance run in the race. The Sailing Committee decided that the *Columbia*'s protest was legitimate, and gave the race to the *Columbia*, making the series tied one-all.

The final and deciding race was called for two days hence, to give the *Bluenose* time to

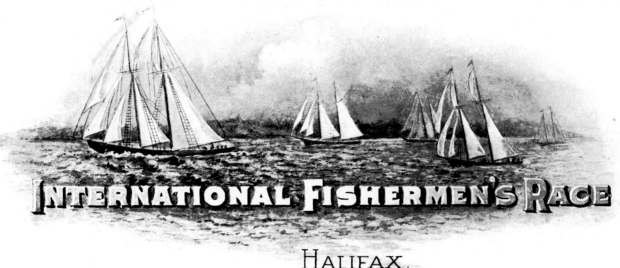

INTERNATIONAL FISHERMEN'S RACE

HALIFAX, CANADA.

Special Rules of 1923
These special rules were brought in immediately following
the 1923 race collision between *Columbia* and *Bluenose*.

1. Passing to windward: An overtaken vessel may luff as she pleases to prevent an overtaking vessel passing her to windward, until she is in such a position that her bowsprit end, or stem if she has no bowsprit, would strike the overtaking vessel abaft the main shrouds, when her right to prevent the other having a free passage to windward shall cease.

2. Passing to leeward: An overtaken vessel must never bear away to prevent another vessel passing her to leeward — the lee side to be considered that on which the leading vessel of the two carries her main boom. The overtaking vessel must not luff until she has drawn clear ahead of the vessel she has overtaken.

3. Rights of new course: A vessel shall not become entitled to her rights on a new course until she has filled away.

4. Passing and rounding marks: If an overlap exists between two vessels when both of them, without tacking, are about to pass a mark on a required side, then the outside vessel must give the inside vessel room to pass clear of the mark. A vessel shall not, however, be justified in attempting to force an overlap and thus force a passage between another vehicle and the mark after the latter has altered her helm for the purpose of rounding.

5. Overlap: An overlap is established when an overtaking vessel has no longer a free choice on which side she will pass, and continues to exist as long as the leeward vessel by luffing, or the weather vessel by bearing away, is in danger of fouling.

6. Obstruction to sea room: When a vessel is approaching a shore, shoal, rock, vessel or other dangerous obstruction, and cannot go clear by altering her course without fouling another vessel, then the latter shall, on behing hailed by the former, at once give room; and in case one vessel is forced to tack or to bear away in order to give room, the other shall also tack or bear away as the case may be, at as near the same time as is possible without danger of fouling. But if such obstruction is a designated mark of the course, a vessel forcing another to tack under the provisions of this section shall be disqualified.

7. If any competing vessel foul a buoy marking the course or foul another competing vessel during the race, she may be disqualified by the Sailing Committee and in the event of disqualification shall score no points in such race.

8. If a vessel crosses the line before the starting gun is fired, her number will be displayed at the end of the "Breakwater" and she will have to return and recross the starting line, otherwise she shall be disqualified from the race.

9. All protests regarding any race shall be made in writing and delivered to the Chairman of the Sailing Committee on the day of the race. Such protests shall be heard and considered by the Sailing Committee and its decision thereon shall be final.

10. Starting and finishing line to be a line from the end of breakwater at Point Pleasant Park, extending easterly across the harbour, and marked by two poles in line on the breakwater.

Vessels starting and finishing must pass between Ives Knoll and Reid Rock Buoys.

19. *Spectators lining Halifax shore line during the 1923 International Fishermen's Race.*

repair a sprung maintopmast, but Walters, refusing to accept the decision of the previous race, left Halifax in protest and headed for Lunenburg. No coaxing would bring him back. Ben Pine, left with the prospect of sailing the course alone to take possession of the Trophy, declined and sailed off to Gloucester, leaving the 1923 series incompleted. The prize money of $5,000 was split between the two schooners, but the disagreement over the ruling caused a break in the International Fisherman's competition that lasted for seven years.

In the next few years the sea took her toll of sailing vessels working on the Atlantic Fishing grounds. The *Columbia* and the sister ship of the *Bluenose*, the *Haligonian*, both ran aground within a week of each other in 1926 and both were hauled off safely. But a year later, in August, the *Columbia*, caught off Sable Island in bad weather, sank with all her crew. The *Henry Ford* was lost the next year off Martin Point, Newfoundland. The boats mentioned were only the most prominent because of their involvement in the International Fisher-

man's Race, but many others followed similar ends. Almost every day the newspapers would relate stories of vessels in distress or missing.

In the storms of April 1926 and August 1927, the Lunenburg fleet was severely battered. One day in April 1926, eight boats returned from the Banks early because of damage from the sea. Among them was the *Bluenose*. She was in relatively good shape, with two anchors lost, 300 fathom of cable missing, all her fishing gear gone, and a badly damaged foresail. The other vessels suffered various injuries and loss of equipment far worse than the *Bluenose*. However, the season had just started, and at the end of April an even fiercer storm hit. This time the *Bluenose* was caught off Northwest Point of Sable Island's southwest exposure during a blinding snowstorm. She had already parted with one anchor, when a great sea swept over forward breaking the second cable, smashing fourteen stanchions and carrying away part of the rail and bulwarks. The only way out was windward working northwest around the point or straight out to sea. For

20. *Well astern of* Bluenose, *the* Haligonian *attempts to gain on her sister ship during the Nova Scotia Fisherman's Race of 1926.*

seven hours under jumbo, double-reefed foresail and a riding sail, she kept biting her way windward into the teeth of the gale in what may be considered the greatest race of her life. The wind finally hauled around a bit to the northwesterly, enough for the *Bluenose* to clear South West Point and carry her crew of twenty to safety.

In the Fall of 1926 two separate races took place. In Gloucester, the *Columbia* and the *Henry Ford* had one last contest between them before both were lost at sea. In two successive events, the *Columbia* outsailed the *Ford*. It was unfortunate that the *Columbia* never had another chance to compete with the *Bluenose*. By watching her sailing capabilities, many people agreed that she was the vessel that would give the *Bluenose* the most challenge. In Halifax a race was arranged between the *Haligonian* and the *Bluenose*. The *Haligonian* was built in Shelbourne in 1925 along the same designs of William Roue as the *Bluenose* and was thought to be a good match. The *Bluenose* took the races, winning by such a long margin that people wondered what was

wrong with the *Haligonian*.

In 1930 another race was held in Gloucester with the *Bluenose* competing against a new schooner, the *Gertrude L. Thebaud*, captained by Walters' old rival Ben Pine. The race was run for the Sir Thomas Lipton Cup. The *Bluenose* lost badly in, perhaps, the worst race of her career. Speculation was made that the *Bluenose* had taken unseen damage after being aground four days off Placentia Bay, Newfoundland, earlier in the year.

In the second race the *Bluenose* rallied her old spirit and led the boat across the finish, but in the third and final race, the *Bluenose* was soundly beaten. Walters reported that they had hit Round Rock Shoal three times but "wouldn't stop and use it as an alibi for defeat." Nor would he "cast any reflections to the three Gloucestermen on board as crew at the time, one who was handling the wheel." New England was jubilant and immediately plans were being made for a return competition to decide the winner of the International Fisherman's Trophy. Due to the lateness of the season and the fact that

The Montreal Daily Star   Wednesday, October 21, 1931.

WELL DONE, BLUENOSE!

Canada: Just wait until I fill the mug, Sam, and
we'll have a loving cup toast to the next race.

the race was funded by public subscription,
the Race Committee decided to leave the race
until next year.

　　After a lapse of seven years, the International Fisherman's Race was revived in 1931.
The *Bluenose* was accepted, unchallenged,
as the Canadian defender. In Gloucester,
after an elimination race with the *Elsie*, the
Gertrude L. Thebaud was chosen as the
American challenger. Captain Walters was
confident of another win, as he quoted a
ten-year-old belief: "The wood is not grown
yet, that will build a boat which will beat the
13 *Bluenose*."

　　The first race took place in Halifax on
October 17, 1931, and although the *Bluenose*
won the race by a very wide margin, the race
exceeded the official time limit of six hours
14 and was called "No race" by the committee.
Two days later in the second race, the
Bluenose appeared to be racing against the
clock and not against the *Thebaud* as she
crossed the finish line a mere six minutes,
eleven seconds ahead of the deadline, with
the *Thebaud* following far behind. The next
race was much closer, and the *Bluenose* beat

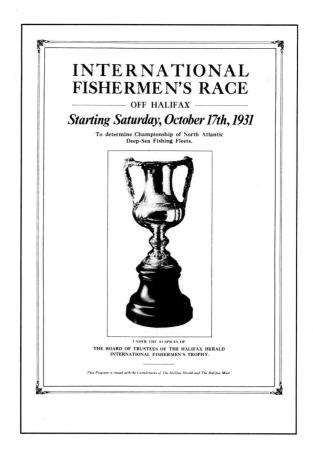

INTERNATIONAL
FISHERMEN'S RACE
— OFF HALIFAX —
Starting Saturday, October 17th, 1931

To determine Championship of North Atlantic
Deep-Sea Fishing Fleets.

UNDER THE AUSPICES OF
THE BOARD OF TRUSTEES OF THE HALIFAX HERALD
INTERNATIONAL FISHERMEN'S TROPHY.

This Program is issued with the Compliments of The Halifax Herald and The Halifax Mail

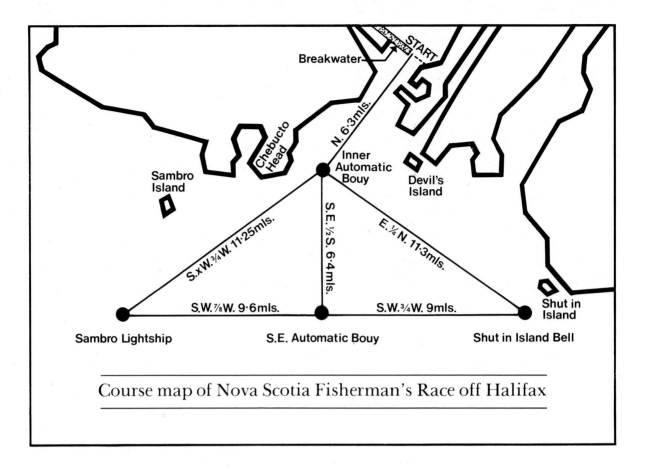

Course map of Nova Scotia Fisherman's Race off Halifax

her rival across the finish by twelve minutes, thus retaining her title as "Queen of the Atlantic Fishing Fleet."

15   In 1932 the fish markets were depressed and many vessels were left to lie alongside their wharfs rather than put out to sea and return with catches that would bring in little or no money. This was the time when the *Bluenose* started her tour as a showboat. If no money could be made fishing, perhaps she could earn something off her name. She had already become a legend across the country, after her likeness was placed upon the Canadian 50¢ stamp in 1928. She was first to represent the Maritime provinces in the Chicago Exposition of 1933. Smartly painted and outfitted, with her fishermen crew dressed in naval uniforms, she started on a voyage into the Great Lakes. Her welcome to ports like Montreal, Toronto, and Chicago was enthusiastic, for her reputation had preceded her. People looked forward to visiting this popular vessel, and they did it by the thousands. The owners of the vessel helped to pay for the trip by organizing charters and cruises. She win-

tered in Toronto and spent part of the next season barnstorming various ports on the Lakes.

At the time of the *Bluenose*'s stay in Chicago, there was a race from that city to Mackinac. The *Bluenose* was too large to participate for the Mackinac Cup, but arrangements were made for her to race alongside the event with any other vessels that cared to join. An alternative prize of a 300-pound American cheese was put up for the first vessel to cross the finish line, regardless of size. Twenty-seven boats competed in the 331-mile race to Mackinac, and the *Bluenose* led the fleet across the finish line, winning the token prize.

In 1935, the *Bluenose* crossed the Atlantic Ocean for the first time to attend the Silver Jubilee of King George V and Queen Mary. During the Spit Head review of the fleet, Captain Walters was invited to visit the King, whereupon the Monarch presented the Captain with a set of sails from the Royal Yacht *Britannia*. The *Bluenose* was also invited to compete in one of the traditional races around the Isle of Wight. Although the

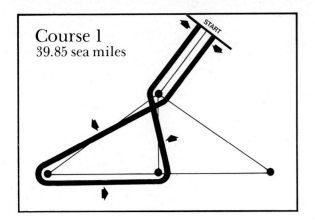

Course 1
39.85 sea miles

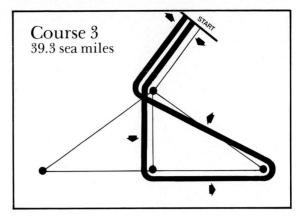

Course 3
39.3 sea miles

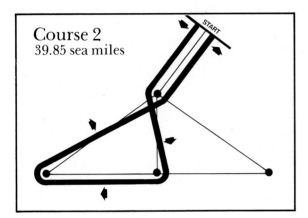

Course 2
39.85 sea miles

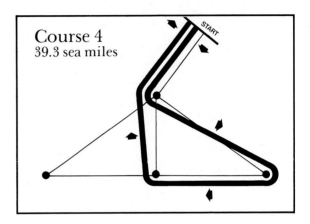

Course 4
39.3 sea miles

Bluenose was not designed for yacht racing, she did put up a good show coming in third after Davis's *Westward* and Runciman's *Altair*.

The *Bluenose* left England in September to sail back to Canada, but two hundred miles from Falmouth she encountered a fierce storm, which laid her over and caused considerable damage. The crew and passengers had to work non-stop to move the iron ballast forward in order to relieve the pounding on the stern. Both lifeboats were smashed, the foreboom, mainboom jaws and part of the bulwarks were carried away, and the galley housing was uprooted. The vessel was forced into Plymouth for a thirty-day layover to effect repairs. She then returned, unhampered, to rejoin the fishing fleet in Lunenburg.

In 1938 the last International Fisherman's Cup race was held off Gloucester and Boston. Many realized this would be the last time they would see a race between such vessels. Fishing under sail had all but ended, replaced by motorized vessels. The newspapers stated, "Power has crowded sail from the fishing fleets. We have seen about the last of the topsails above the headlands. It is all oil today in Nova Scotian fishing ports that used to know the forests of tall spars and towering canvas of the Banks schooner." Even the *Bluenose* was forced to compete with this new age by having twin diesels installed in 1936 at the cost of $12,000. And most vessels that had competed in the Fisherman's Race were lost, the *Elsie* having sprung a leak and sunk off St. Pierre in 1935, leaving her crew to row forty-eight miles to shore. No longer were the big Banks schooners being constructed.

The *Bluenose* motored into Gloucester on October 2, 1938, seventeen years old and showing signs of strain. She was old and her qualities uncertain after so many years at sea. She was most certainly hogged, the bow and stern sagging slightly from the middle. Ten years was usually the normal working life of a salt-banker, after which the boat was abandoned or sold for coastal trade. She spent one week having her engines removed and her gear outfitted and repaired for the race. With her rival of eight years, the

16

21. Gertrude L. Thebaud *was the longest rival of* Bluenose, *defeating the latter in the Sir Thomas* Lipton Cup race of 1930, but losing to Bluenose *in the two remaining International Fisherman's Cup races.*

Gertrude L. Thebaud, they sailed to Boston where the first race was to be held.

The first race was held on October 9 on an eighteen-mile course which was to be circled twice. The *Thebaud* established a good lead on the first round and held onto it, crossing the finish line two minutes, fifty-six seconds ahead of the *Bluenose*. The Canadian vessel had fractured her foretopmast during the race and was forced to dowse her jibtop and foretopsails. This was the first of the many mishaps that the *Bluenose* encountered during the series. Captain Walters protested
17 that the "merry-go-round" course was not fit for fishermen. The committee "tried to mollify the peppery Angus Walters . . . that they were trying to protect the vessels from
18 the dangers of twelve miles off shore." Walters reminded them that "the *Bluenose* and the *Thebaud* were accustomed not to waters twelve miles from land, but hundreds, and that the racing committee's
19 concern was not appreciated." The next race did not occur until the 13th, because the weather had been considered too light. The *Bluenose* found her speed in the lighter airs

and drifted across the finish line almost twelve minutes ahead of her rival. During the second half of the race, the *Bluenose* blew her staysail in half and had to replace it with a smaller one until the first could be repaired.

Several days later the next race was staged. In the meantime Ben Pine became ill with sinus trouble and was replaced by Captain Cecil Moulton. The *Thebaud* was taken out of the water because it was found that her old paint was peeling off in giant strips and causing drag. The race on the 20th was run over a smooth sea and the *Thebaud* beat the *Bluenose* by a mile, but they had exceeded the official time limit of five hours, so it was
20 declared "No Race."

There was concern that the crew of the *Bluenose* had been shifting ballast between races because it was found that over three hundred ingots had been moved onto the *Bluenose* from the dockside. This activity contravened the regulations under the "Deed of Gift." The *Bluenose*'s trim was poor and had been commented upon during the races. Her ballast when built was seventy tons, but

22. *Her head down and decks awash, the crew of the*
Gertrude L. Thebaud *struggle with the mainsail*
halyards.

after seventeen years at sea had been reduced to about fifty tons. It was common knowledge that the crew had been shifting ballast, but the press got wind of the story and caused an uproar. The head of the Race Committee, Captain Lyons, brushed aside the protest saying, "I told them to get their boats to the waterline required by the 'Deed of Gift' and I don't care how they do it."

21

The *Bluenose* was measured and found to be too deep on the waterline, so a lighting plant, air tank, and five tons of oil were removed. The *Bluenose*, now lighter, was found to handle far better. In the light winds of the next race on October 23, she had her second victory over the *Thebaud*, crossing the finish line six minutes and thirty-nine seconds ahead of her rival. On the following day, the fourth race was run on a 35½ irregular triangle off Nahant Bay. The *Thebaud* handled well in the boisterous seas, but the *Bluenose* had trouble with her gear. Her backstay parted and caused her to come up into the wind, leaving the *Thebaud* to speed ahead and take the race by five minutes.

Storm warnings postponed the next race for a day and on October 26 the last race was held. Light winds forced postponement early in the day and finally at 12:05 the gun sounded the start to the race. The *Bluenose* sailed well in the light winds and held onto the lead throughout the race. As she neared the finish her topsail halyard block gave way, but she was too near victory to be stopped and crossed the finish line in 4:04:10, followed by the *Thebaud* in 4:07:00, giving the race and the final championship to the *Bluenose*.

All the Captains were upset with the progress of the series. Captain Moulton asserted, "The *Thebaud* was not beaten by the *Bluenose*, but by Captain Lyons [head of the Race committee]. He sent us out day after day when there wasn't enough wind for a real race and kept us in port when there

22 was a good wind." Captain Pine stated that he would not challenge again. "We took two races sailed in a good breeze. The *Bluenose* took three in weather I don't consider fit for

23 a fisherman's race." And Captain Walters told reporters that "the *Bluenose,* as long as

23. The Bluenose *off the Isle of Wight, 1935.*

I am Master, will never race again in the United States."

Captain Moulton, dismayed by the outcome of the races, sent a telegram to Captain Walters: "I hearby challenge you to a race in Massachusetts waters over your own course in any breeze of twenty-five knots or over, you and I put up $500 each and race vessels under 'Deed of Gift.' Please advise immediately. Put up or shut up. Winnings go to the winning crew." Walters replied to the telegram stating that he had "more important personal things to think about." And indeed he had, for he was returning home to Nova Scotia to be married. But Walters could not resist a further challenge and he replied the next day to the presss: "Five hundred dollars, bah! That's only poker-chip money those Gloucester people are talking about. Let's get this thing settled for once and for all. Let's race for $5,000, from Boston to Bermuda, around the island and back to Halifax, winner take all. Let them think that over instead of spouting chicken feed." Neither challenge was accepted.

In the middle of all this the International Trophy was stolen. It had been on display in a Boston department-store window, but when time came to retrieve it, the cup was missing. It was thought to be the work of pranksters, and this was confirmed three days later when the coveted Trophy was found on the steps of a foundling home with a poem attached.

> Here's to Angus, good old sport,
> Whose challenge sort of takes us short.
> Send us a gale that blows at Thirty,
> And we'd bet our shirts on little Gerty.

There also appeared to be some question of the prize money, as it was not available at the Cup presentation. In fact, it took some months to recover it with the help of lawyers, so Walters, sarcastically, ordered the *Bluenose* to return home "before she too disappeared." The Trophy was presented and Captain Walters returned to Lunenburg. Both he and his crew were received in grand style, celebrations were held, and the *Bluenose* feats were lauded. The Lunenburgers even replied to the Gloucester poem with one of their own:

23a

And here's to Gerty, who tried in vain,
The Fisherman's trophy to regain.
The Bermuda challenge she also shirks,
So make better use of your Yankee shirts.

30

The excitement was not to last. The *Bluenose* was not in demand as a fisherman; she was in debt for payment on her engines; war was brewing in Europe; and attention quickly became focused elsewhere. She sat idle at a Lunenburg wharf until put under the Auctioneer's hammer in 1939. But Walters attempted to forestall the inevitable by putting up $7,000 to take full possession of the *Bluenose* and by trying to spark public interest in her preservation. Times were against the old vessel. She was of no use or interest, so in 1942 the *Bluenose* was sold for coastal trading in the Caribbean to the West Indian Trading Company. With World War II at its height, large motorized vessels were prime targets for submarines, but small vessels like the *Bluenose* went by virtually unnoticed. Under the command of Captain Beringers, the *Bluenose* spent the next few years shipping needed supplies to the islands of the West Indies.

Navigation in the postwar Caribbean was tricky at best, systems of buoyage and lights were not in extensive use, and the tides varied greatly. During a dark January night in 1946, the *Bluenose* overran her time and distance. At 7:20 p.m. the lookout yelled that there was water breaking ahead. The warning was too late. Minutes later, the *Bluenose* struck a reef off Ile à Vache, Haiti. She was wrecked beyond repair, her keel was broken, and she was split completely across her breakbeam, with water flooding her interior. The crew managed to lower boats and put ashore safely. The next day they found the *Bluenose* still clinging to the reef. Help was found and they returned to the schooner to salvage what they could. The precious diesel engines were hauled out and brought ashore. Later the *Bluenose* slid off the reef and onto the bottom.

It is perhaps fitting that the *Bluenose*'s oldest rival sank not far away in the Caribbean. The *Gertrude L. Thebaud* rammed a breakwater and sank in the port of La Guadera, Venezuela, in 1948.

BLUENOSE II

Eight
colour portraits
of Bluenose II

24. *"Mainsail Up."*

25. *Raising topsails in Halifax Harbour.*

26. Bow lookout in heavy fog.

27. *Crew bending on jib topsail.*

28. *Looking aft through the main peak halyards.*

29. *Bras d'Or Lakes at sunrise.*

30. *Under full sail in Halifax Harbour.*

31. Early morning Bras d'Or Lake.

32. *Looking aloft to the ratlines and headsails.*

33. *The mainsail measures 4,100 square feet, and is
secured to an 81-foot boom.*

34. *Sails full and drawing well.*

35. *Jumbo, jib, and jib topsail.*

"Mainsail Up," orders the Captain and the crew moves into their position. Throat and peak halyards are run up forward to the windlass. Stops are taken off the massive sail, and it slides and unfolds upon the accommodation roof. Quarter tackles are removed from the boom, and the crutch is taken away as the main gaff moves slowly skyward, pulling with it the great expanse of the mainsail. The helmsman holds the vessel into the wind as the mainsail is raised to its great height, and the halyards are stopped off and tied to the pinrail and the sheet is run out to a determined position. The crew then move forward to raise the foresail and they repeat the same procedure. Next come the jumbo and jib. Willing hands grasp the halyards and haul the sails upwards, the metal hanks making a skating sound as one follows another up the metal stay from the bowsprit.

More sail is unfurled and raised. Figures scamper up the ratlines and loose the topsails from their stowage against the topmasts and the sail billows out with the wind. The jib topsail is loosened from the bowsprit and raised, and the crew moves below to the hold and bring another sail to the deck. The fisherman's staysail is secured to the halyards and hauled up between the masts.

The Captain nods to the helmsman and indicates a course heading. The ship's head pulls round quickly as the wind begins to fill the sails and the vessel begins to speak. Blocks creak, halyards pop and crack as they tighten around their pins, and the wood-work of the hull and masts groan slightly as a tremendous strain comes upon the vessel. The boat heels gently and the rudder bites, as the vessel starts moving forward in the light swell. The bow gently rising and falling as the cutwater begins to hiss a watery sound as a bone of white water is formed in her teeth.

Many years had passed since that winter day in January 1946 when an announcer's voice came over the air reporting the loss of the *Bluenose*, wrecked on a reef in the distant Caribbean. Nova Scotians felt the loss deeply. With hardly a comment, they had let a proud part of their heritage leave

36. *Overlooking the foredeck from the mainmast.*

37. *Departing Halifax for foreign waters.*

the province. They had quickly forgotten the vessel, as world issues took precedence. With her destruction she was strongly remembered, but it was not until long after the war that the idea of building a replica was entertained. In 1960, in Lunenburg, Nova Scotia, at the Smith and Rhuland Shipyard, a project was begun that was to become an inspiration for that idea. A ship was being built, a wooden replica of H.M.S. *Bounty*, for the movie production of M.G.M.'s *Mutiny on the Bounty*. The public watched on with interest as the keel was laid and the wooden frames took shape. By the time the vessel was launched, most people could not help thinking that this could have been the *Bluenose*.

Committees were then formed to study the idea of building a replica of the *Bluenose*, but even the most ardent supporters of the scheme soon realized that the cost of construction would be enormous and the amount of money necessary would be extremely difficult if not impossible to raise. It was fortunate that the brewing firm of Oland and Sons was planning a somewhat

similar project. The company had the idea of building a replica of a Nova Scotian fishing schooner (to be called the *Olands Schooner*) to promote their new product, Schooner Beer. When Olands became aware of the interest in Lunenburg of reconstructing the *Bluenose*, they decided to build the replica themselves. With the enthusiastic approval of the people of Nova Scotia, the project was soon begun.

The Olands decided the replica should bear every resemblance to the original in hull, rigging, and sail plan, but the interior should be altered to accommodate passengers. The *Bluenose II* would not fish or race, as did her predecessor, but would earn a living carrying passengers. Months were spent researching documents and photographs. Old shipwrights and sailors were interviewed, and many were brought out of retirement to work on the new vessel. Both Captain Angus Walters and the designer William Roue were consulted and the designer's plans were made available. After alterations were made on the drawing board, construction was ready to begin.

The keel was laid on February 27, 1963, and five months later the vessel was ready to be launched. The public watched on eagerly as the famous hull took shape in the Smith and Rhuland yard. On July 24, 1963, amid a cheering throng of 15,000 who crowded the waterfront to watch the event, the *Bluenose II* was christened, and her sleek black hull slipped gracefully into the waters of Lunenburg harbour. For one man who stood on her deck as the boat was launched, it must have been a particularly fulfilling moment. Captain Angus Walters, the eighty-two-year-old master of the original *Bluenose*, must have felt profound delight to have his old charge come back to life after so many years.

The *Bluenose* now sailed back into the daily life of the people of Nova Scotia. In a harbour which once contained hundreds of masts, the *Bluenose* reappeared to bring back a flood of memories from a not-so-distant past. A proud memory had returned to life.

Upon the Olands' direction, the *Bluenose II* spent the next six years involved in the passenger trade. From the recently acquired wharf in Halifax, the vessel took out deck passengers on daily cruises during the summer. In the winter the *Bluenose II* headed south to the Caribbean where she had established herself in the charter business from a base in English Harbour, Antigua. During these years she was commanded by Captain Elsworth Coggins, whose experience with sail included the replica H.M.S. *Bounty*.

Her first charter was one of romantic adventure. She was hired by an American film company to take an expedition to an island in the Pacific Ocean in search of treasure. Three hundred miles off the Panama coast the *Bluenose II* anchored at Cocos Island where a pirate by the name of Benito who had looted Peruvian churches in the 1820's had apparently buried his plunder. The vessel acted as a base camp for the searchers and the film crew. After weeks of fruitless searching the expedition packed up and the *Bluenose II* headed back to the Caribbean to resume further charters. A film was produced by Taylor Television called "Expedition Bluenose."

38. *Preparing to raise her mainsail.*

In 1967 the *Bluenose II* headed up the St. Lawrence River on a trip that was reminiscent of her predecessor's history. In 1933 the Bluenose had been invited to the Chicago Exposition; thirty-four years later the *Bluenose II* was invited to the World's Fair in Montreal. She stayed for six months, acting officially as host vessel to Expo 67, welcoming visitors arriving to the site by boat or ship.

In 1971 the ownership of the *Bluenose II* changed. The Oland family decided that they no longer wished to operate the boat and offered to turn her over to the province. The Nova Scotia Government accepted, and on September 7, 1971, the Olands formally ''sold'' the *Bluenose II* to the province for the amount of one dollar.

Rumours had circulated that the vessel was suffering from dry rot, and a marine survey soon verified this. The *Bluenose II* needed an extensive refit to replace the affected areas and to check further rotting. To help underwrite the $250,000 refit, the Nova Scotia government started a nationwide ''Save the *Bluenose*'' campaign. The reaction to the plea was truly admirable; thousands of schoolchildren across the country donated their ''Bluenose'' dimes; small businesses and larger companies poured in money; and eventually $155,000 was raised from public subscription, the rest covered by the government in the form of work grants.

By 1973 the *Bluenose II* was once again sailing the waters of Nova Scotia. Under the new command of Captain Skodge, who had been first mate with Captain Coggins, the vessel was ready to embark on a new role under provincial direction. During that summer the *Bluenose II* engaged in a similar schedule of harbour tours as before, and also made various trips to ports about the province so the public could enjoy a first-hand look at their newly acquired vessel. The government had no desire to re-enter the charter trade in the south, as had the Olands, so in winter the boat lay idle at Olands' wharf.

The next year the *Bluenose II* made her first major voyage as ambassador of Nova Scotia. She sailed south to Norfolk, Virginia,

39. *While sitting at her berth at Historic Properties, the crew loads one of the six twenty-person life rafts on board.*

and then worked her way up the Eastern Seaboard, visiting all the major American ports along the way. With her arrival at each port, thousands of visitors would come down to inspect the vessel. The *Bluenose II* became an ideal symbol for promoting tourism to the province. The 1974 trip marked the start of a regular season of events for the next few years. At the beginning of each new season, the schooner would head out on a promotional tour outside the province; in the summer she would return to Halifax for two months of harbour tours; and in the fall she would set sail for different ports about the province to participate in local fairs and exhibitions and to sail further tours from these ports. In October she would be laid up for the winter and refitted for the coming season.

In the Spring of 1975, the *Bluenose II* set sail from Halifax for a second journey up the St. Lawrence River and into the Great Lakes. This six-week cruise up into the interior of Canada and the United States was purely a promotional tour to stimulate tourism to the province of Nova Scotia.

With Captain E. Hartling as the newly appointed master, the schooner made an immensely successful journey. She headed up the river, stopping at Quebec, Montreal, Kingston, Cornwall, through the canal system and down along the American shore of Lake Erie to Buffalo, Erie, Toledo, Cleveland, Detroit, and back into Canadian waters at Windsor, where she then returned to Toronto and home.

The response to her visits was overwhelmingly enthusiastic. An estimated crowd of over one hundred thousand people walked over her decks during the six-week period. At each port dozens of small craft, blowing horns and sirens, would escort the *Bluenose II* into her berth; and upon her arrival a band was usually waiting, ready to strike up a welcome tune. The whole cruise was one of festive occasions, because people in the ports around the Lakes did not often have a chance to see a tall-rigged ship enter their harbour. Some spectators even brought along souvenirs of the original *Bluenose*, which had sailed there in 1933, and they asked for autographs from the crew of the

40. Bluenose II *and the* Pride of Baltimore.

Bluenose II to go alongside the 1933 signatures. All and all the trip to the Lakes showed how extremely interested people were in the ship, her crew, and her history.

On her return to Nova Scotia, the *Bluenose II* was welcomed in Halifax by a band and large crowd for the official opening of her new berth. This was constructed at Historic Properties, a collection of ancient privateering warehouses which had been recently restored. The schooner fit perfectly into the new harbour-front development, with her tall spars towering over buildings three hundred years old.

In 1976 the *Bluenose II* was invited to participate in the gala Bi-Centennial Celebrations in the United States. With Captain E. Hartling as master, the schooner set sail from Halifax in early spring and headed south on an extensive visit to American seaports. She sailed first to New Orleans and then proceeded to move north up the Eastern Seaboard of the United States to New York City. Unfortunately during the trip a disagreement developed between Captain

Hartling and the Nova Scotia government over the carrying of a passenger. Regulations did not allow passengers to accompany the ship on foreign cruises. The dispute ended with Hartling's dismissal and replacement by Captain Andrew Thomas. Under new command, the *Bluenose II* sailed into New York harbour on July 4 to be part of Operation Sail, the greatest amalgamation of tall ships to be gathered together this century. Sailing ships of all descriptions from all over the world were invited to New York City for a sail past in honour of the United State's two-hundredth anniversary. Awards were presented for a vessel's appearance, and the *Bluenose II* was awarded "Second Smartest Vessel" in her class. The *Winston Churchill* of the United Kingdom had taken first prize.

Her next major cruise was in 1978 under the command of Captain Don Barr, who had taken over from Captain Thomas when he resigned the previous year. Captain Barr began his career on the *Bluenose II* as a seaman and worked his way up through bosun and first mate to become the master of

41. *Under full sail in a light breeze.*

42. Filmstrip of her maiden voyage shows the helmsman struggling to keep the schooner steady in the heavy seas.

the schooner. In early spring, the vessel sailed to Bermuda for ten days to paint and varnish her brightwork, then sailed to Tampa, Dry Tortugas, Fort Lauderdale, Savannah, Wilmington, Norfolk, Annapolis, Baltimore, Philadelphia, New York, New London, and Gloucester before returning home to Halifax where she resumed her role running harbour tours for the tourist industry.

The *Bluenose II* has become a part of the Nova Scotian way of life. She does not play the same role of that of her predecessor, but she still represents a bygone era. For the people who sit on her deck or watch from the shore as she raises her massive sail, it does not take very much imagination to find themselves dreaming of a different time and what life was once like. For those thoughts alone the vessel has earned a well-respected place in her community, for she gives future generations a sense of history.

*43. Weathering hurricane-force winds under reefed
foresail during her maiden voyage.*

44. Crewmen lashing the mainsail to the boom.

45. Rounding Cape Breton on a cold, wet morning in May, Bluenose II makes her way towards the St. Lawrence River.

46. *For safety the helmsman is tied to his position at the wheel.*

47. *Toward the St. Lawrence River via Cape Breton.*

48. *Lashings being secured to the jib and jib topsail.*

49. *The crew consists of a Captain, first mate, bosun,*
Chief Engineer, cook, steward, and ten seamen.

51. *Hull planking being replaced during a winter's refit on the La Have River.*

50. *Sitting high out of water during an annual inspection, the schooner prepares for another season.*

The keel was made of hardwoods. From the keel sixty-three pairs of frames were raised. The frames, made of oak and birch, were doubled around twenty-seven-inch centers and formed the shape of the hull. A spruce keelson was installed above the keel and on top of the frames. Long bolts were passed through the keel, frame, and keelson and drawn tight; this clamped the frames securely into position. The exterior planking was then added to form the outside hull. Hardwoods were used below the waterline and spruce and Douglas fir above. The planking was secured to the frames with thousands of wooden nails called treenails. Planking of spruce was set into place on the interior side of the frames to form a double skin on the hull to increase the strength.

With the hull completed, the deck began to take shape. Spruce shelves were set on either side of the vessel and ran the entire length. Deck beams of spruce were laid upon the shelves and moulded to give the deck its camber. Smaller beams called carlings were then laid in a fore and aft line between the beams to form a gridwork for the deck

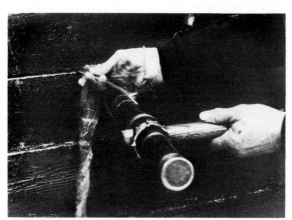

52. *Driving in oakum with time-honoured practice, the seams are made watertight.*

53. *Manila is used for the main and fore sheets.*

planking of clear pine to be laid. The carlings and beams would also form the support around openings in the deck for accommodation housing and hatches. The deck housings were of mahogany.

The interior of the vessel is a vast departure from the original *Bluenose*. In the stern accommodation is a modern chart-room and six walnut panelled staterooms, each with two berths. Forward of the accommodation is the engine room contain-ing the vessels main propulsion and generating systems. Next to the engine room is the ship's hold. The hold is used to stow extra sail, ship's gear, and refrigeration and laundry facilities as well as two small cabins with two berths each. Past the hold and moving forward is the salon which is used for dining and social functions. Forward of the salon is the galley, crew's mess with one small two-berth cabin on the port side and the forecastle with eight bunks for the crew. The salon, hold, engine room, and forward section of the after-accommodation would have been the location of the fish hold in the original *Bluenose*.

After the hull was sanded, caulked and painted, the *Bluenose II* was launched. She was then taken to a fitter's wharf, where her mast and rigging were installed. All the masts, booms, and gaffs were made of Douglas fir and the bowsprit of spruce. Great care was taken to rig the ship like the original, although there were certain changes and additions. On the foremast is a large white dome, which would have seemed mysterious to sailors of the Twenties, for it contains the ship's radar. The sails were first made of canvas but were eventually changed to dacron. Polypropylene rope is used in many places because synthetic rope is more readily available than good grade manila. A power windlass was added to the forward part of the vessel and smaller ones were placed under the mainmast and at the stern. These were added to lessen the manpower needed to raise the main and foresails, handling of sheets, and could also be used to raise the anchor and assist in mooring. The sails are raised and lowered through a system of blocks and tackle identical to the original *Bluenose*.

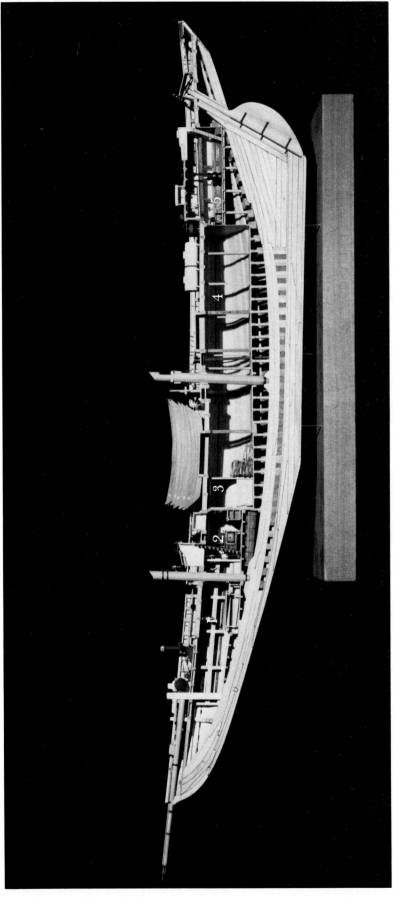

54. *Interior of Bluenose.*

1. Crews Accommodation
   and Mess

2. Galley

3. Salt Hold

4. Fish Hold

5. Masters Accommodation

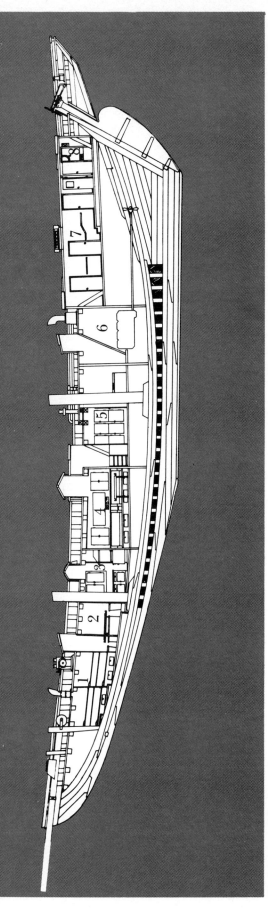

55. *Interior of Bluenose II.*

1. Crews Accommodation
2. Crews Mess
3. Galley
4. Main Salon
5. Ships Hold
6. Engine Room
7. After Accommodation
8. Chart Room

Bluenose II Specifications

Length Overall	143 ft.		Total Overall	108 ft.	
Waterline Length	112 ft.		Foreboom	32 ft. 10 in.	
Outside Plank Beam	27 ft.		Fore Gaff	33 ft. 2 in.	
Load Draught	16 ft. 6 in.		Mainmast Diameter at Step	22 in.	
Bowsprit Projection	17 ft. 6 in.		Mainmast Length, Heel to Head	96 ft. 2 in.	
Bowsprit Overall	34 ft.		Main Topmast Length	52 ft. 5 in.	
Jumbo Boom	29 ft.		Total Overall	125 ft. 10 in.	
Foremast Diameter at Step	20 in.		Main Boom	81 ft. 11 in.	
Foremast Length Heel to Head	82 ft. 2 in.		Main Gaff	52 ft. 5 in.	
Foretopmast Length	50 ft. 3 in.		Jib Topsail	1,160 sq. ft.	

Jib	905 sq. ft.		Displacement Tonnage	285.00 T.
Jumbo	655 sq. ft.		Main Propulsion	
Foresail	1,480 sq. ft.		Twin Screw: 2-180 HP Caterpillar Engines	
Fore Gaff-topsail	580 sq. ft.		Generators	
Fisherman's Staysail	1,900 sq. ft.		1-75 KW Caterpillar Generator	
Mainsail	4,100 sq. ft.		1-50 KW Caterpillar Generator	
Main Gaff-topsail	910 sq. ft.		Navigation Equipment	
Total Sail Area	11,690 sq. ft.		Decca Navigator, Loran C. Radar, Depth	
Gross Tonnage	190.48 T.		Sounder, VHF & SSB Communications,	
Registered Tonnage	96.48 T.		Radio Direction Finder	

56. Bluenose in 1935.

PHOTO BEKIN OF COWES

57. Bluenose II in 1976.

58. *Crew members slipping oak hoops around the
mainmast while bending on the mainsail.*

59. *Stepping in a new spruce bowsprit.*

60. *Fixing a position off a distant coast.*

61. *The traditional magnetic compass the helmsman uses to make his course.*

62. *The chartroom containing modern electronic navigational aids.*

63. *The main salon.*

64. Early morning on the La Have River.

65. Winters refit at Snyder's Shipyard at Dayspring, N.S.

66. *A view from astern under full sail.*

Footnote Sources

1. *The Evening Mail,* October 19, 1920.

2. *The Evening Mail,* October 20, 1920.

3. *The Evening Mail,* October 21, 1920.

4. *The Halifax Herald,* October 19, 1921.

5. *The Halifax Herald,* October 24, 1921.

6. *The Halifax Herald,* September 15, 1922.

7. *The Halifax Herald,* September 26, 1922.

8. *The Halifax Herald,* October 8, 1922.

9. *The Halifax Herald,* October 11, 1922.

10. *The Halifax Herald,* October 23, 1922.

11. *The Evening Mail,* October 20, 1930.

12. *The Evening Mail,* October 20, 1930.

13. *The Halifax Herald,* October 15, 1931.

14. *The Halifax Herald,* October 19, 1931.

15. *The Halifax Herald,* October 21, 1931.

16. *The Halifax Herald,* October 27, 1938.

17. *The Halifax Herald,* October 11, 1938.

18. *The Halifax Herald,* October 11, 1938.

19. *The Halifax Herald,* October 11, 1938.

20. *The Halifax Herald,* October 21, 1938.

21. *The Halifax Herald,* October 21, 1938.

22. *The Halifax Herald,* October 27, 1938.

23. *The Halifax Herald,* October 27, 1938.

24. *The Halifax Herald,* October 27, 1938.

25. *The Halifax Herald,* October 28, 1938.

26. *The Halifax Herald,* October 28, 1938.

27. *The Halifax Herald,* October 29, 1938.

28. *The Halifax Herald,* October 30, 1938.

29. *The Halifax Herald,* October 29, 1938.

30. *The Halifax Herald,* November 4, 1938.

Photograph Credits

Maritime Museum of the Atlantic 22, 23a

F.W. Wallace Collection, Maritime Museum of the Atlantic .... 6, 12 & 13, 4, 5, 8

Beken of Cowes, Isle of Wight, England 1, 23, 56

Albert M. Barnes Collection, The Mariners' Museum, Newport News, Virginia 7, 11

The Mariners' Museum, Newport News, Virginia 3, 16, 15

Peabody Museum of Salem, Massachusetts 14

H.E. Keniston Collection 17, 21

R. Walker Collection 2, 10, 9, 20

Nova Scotia Communications and Information 40

U.S. Coast Guard 43

Ontario Science Centre 54

Canadian Broadcasting Corporation .... End paper photograph, Film strip 18

C.V. Cooke and Associates Ltd. 19

R. Keith McLaren: All colour photographs, Line drawing 55, Photographs 32-39, 41, 44-53, 57-66

Acknowledgements

Nova Scotia Department of Tourism

Public Archives of Nova Scotia

Nova Scotia Museum

Maritime Museum of the Atlantic

Nova Scotia College of Art and Design

Boston Public Library

Photo 67

Captain Don Barr, Bluenose II

Ben Verburgh, Ontario Science Centre

Graham and Nita Lavers

Vivian Cameron

Jo Anna Issak

Ned Norwood

References

Andrew Merkel, *Schooner Bluenose*, The Ryerson Press, 1948.

Jerry Gilespie, *Bluenose Skipper*, Brunswick Press, 1955.

Brian and Phil Backman, *Bluenose*, McClelland & Stewart, 1964.

Howard Chapelle, *The American Fishing Schooner 1825-1935*, Norton Press, 1973.

Sterling Hayden, *Wanderer*, Alfred A. Knopf Inc., 1963.

L.B. Jenson, *Bluenose II, Last of the Tall Schooners*, Bluenose Designs, 1975.

F.W. Wallace, *The Roving Fisherman*, Canadian Fisherman, 1955.

Albert Church and John Connolly, *The American Fisherman*, Bonanza Books, 1940.

John Connolly, *Gloucester Fisherman*, The John Day Company, 1927.

The Halifax Herald, The Evening Mail, The Boston Herald (1919-1938).

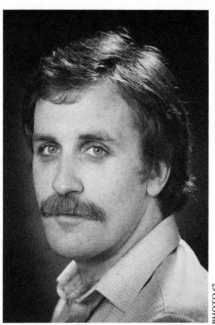

PHOTO 67

Keith McLaren has worked on a wide variety of ships, from tramp steamers to drill ships, as seaman and second mate. During 1975 and 1976 he sailed on the *Bluenose II* as a crewmember. Since his early years he has had a love for photography which he further studied at the Nova Scotia College of Art and Design. He took most of the photographs in the *Bluenose II* section of this book as well as researching and writing the complete text. Keith makes his home in Halifax.